THE FOURTH I WESSEX WALKIES for you and your dog

Dedicated to my dog Bounty, Sharp's successor Laddie and not forgetting Joan Loader (without who's help this book could not have been written)

Patricia M Wilnecker

1998

By the same author

non-fiction
High Street Murders 1598
Published by Poole Museum Services

A History of Upper Parkstone (beginning to 1939)
Upper Parkstone in the Second World War
More Recollections of Old Upper Parkstone
Bounty, the tale of a dog
Wessex Walkies for you and your dog
More Wessex Walkies for you and your dog
Ghostly Tales of Wessex
Even More Wessex Walkies
Published by Patricia M Wilnecker

fiction:
The Bountifull Gyfte
Published by Patricia M Wilnecker

Published by Patricia M Wilnecker
73 Gwynne Road
Parkstone
Poole
Dorset
BH12 2AR

First Published 1998

British Library Cataloguing in Publication Data
A catalogue record for this book is available from the British Library

ISBN 0 9513971 9 2

Made and printed in Great Britain by the Local History Press, 3 Devonshire Promenade, Lenton, Nottingham NG7 2DS

CONTENTS

INTRODUCTION

More Walks for caring dog-owners! I said I wouldn't write another 'walkie' book but we keep finding attractive places that we want to share with you — so here we go again!

FOOD

The places listed are not necessarily starting points for the walks but are within reasonable distance by car. At my last visit — and pleasant though it would be I cannot check every pub frequently! — all the places listed allowed dogs on leads at least for bar meals. However, you may find there has been a change of landlord and perhaps also their attitude to dogs. Having said that, Bounty and I have so far been welcome in all of them as have other dog-owners — so good luck!

CAUTION

Please keep dogs on leads when near livestock. Farmers have the right to shoot loose dogs. Lastly, please do not allow fouling of footpaths or public places.

The information in this book was correct at the time of writing but I am sure you will appreciate it takes a long time to do all these walks, so please let me know if you meet any changes.

ONCE AGAIN, HAPPY WALKIES!

WALK 1 NETLEY, VICTORIA COUNTRY PARK

DURATION: *Flexible*

STARTING POINT: *just before main entrance on right hand side*

FOOD: *Tea rooms in park. Dogs outside only*

From Junction 8 of the M27 follow the brown tourist signs to Victoria Country Park. Leave your car just before the main entrance on the right where there is free parking overlooking the shore. If full, there is a pay and display car park inside. There are acres of parkland to explore but it is worth starting off along the concrete sea wall with great views across Southampton Water and Fawley, then enter the park by the sailing club. To the northwest is squirrel territory, with woods and a stream — a dogs paradise. There is also a miniature railway and the Hamble Rail Trail to explore. You may be curious about the tower and chapel at the centre of the park. They are all that remain of a huge military hospital, demolished in 1966 but the tower is still a landmark for shipping.

WALK 2 BURLEY 'WATERHOLE'

DURATION: *Flexible*
STARTING POINT: *Burley to Thorney Hill road*
FOOD: *Burley Manor Hotel*

To the west of Burley on the road to Thorney Hill just past Burbush House and over to your left is the 'waterhole' where forest ponies and cattle gather. A couple of paths lead to it through heather and gorse and with your dog under control it is possible to observe the wildlife of the New Forest from here. A few hundred yards towards Burley and opposite the car park a pleasant, longer walk can be taken alongside the old railway line and into the wood. If you drive on to Thorney Hill you will see an unusual and interesting church, 'All Saints' on your right. To me it would seem to be more in place in Austria than the New Forest.

WALK 3 'NAKED MAN', WILVERLEY PLAIN

DURATION: *Flexible*
STARTING POINT: *Wilverley Inclosure (toilets)*
FOOD: *White Buck, Burley; Old Station Tearooms, Holmsley (not Mon.) dogs o/s only but some tables under cover*

From the A35 Christchurch to Lyndhurst road turn left at Holmsley and immediately after the Old Station Tearooms turn sharp right to New Milton. The road is built on the old railway line and after about 1 mile bears left. You will soon see the car park on the left, after the sign 'Barbecue Scouts'(!) where the woodland ends and the heath begins. Follow the edge of the wood and after about three quarters of a mile you will see the 'Naked Man', an old, dead tree behind a wooden fence. (It was once a gibbet where smugglers and highwaymen were hanged.) You could continue on the other side of the A35 following footpaths for about one and a half miles and you will see the White Buck signposted. There are many variations to this walk but lead restrictions apply in the Inclosure to safeguard the wildlife.

WALK 4 STUDLAND COMMON, MILFORD ON SEA

DURATION: *Flexible*

STARTING POINT: *Westminster Road from the clifftop.*

FOOD: *Smugglers Inn, Milford on Sea; The Gun Inn, Keyhaven*

If there is no room in Westminster Road there is a pay and display car park on the clifftop. Walk from Westminster Road into Pless Road (from October to April there is unrestricted parking here, too) and immediately opposite the end of Westminster Road you will see a five bar gate and the entrance to Studland Common. There is a sign by the New Forest District Council which declares this to be a place for peace and quiet enjoyment. Cross the field which may contain horses so dogs under control please and follow the path which takes you to a rabbit-nibbled turf area surrounded by blackthorn — a picture in the Spring. There are paths to explore here but if you go straight ahead you will join up with the Danes Stream walk (see *Even More Wessex Walkies*, Walk 12). For the main part of the common however, turn right into an open grassy area with some gorse bushes and a seat where you can rest awhile and let your dog explore.

WALK 5 STURT POND, MILFORD ON SEA

DURATION: *Flexible*

STARTING POINT: *Grebe Close*

FOOD: *Smugglers Inn, Milford on Sea; Gun Inn, Keyhaven*

Park in Grebe Close, just past Swallow Drive by an open grassy area which leads to the pond. There are seats along the way where you can watch the birdlife. The wall passes reedbeds and a caravan site, leading eventually to Hurst Spit, a bank of pebbles extending to Hurst Castle which was built in the time of Henry VIII to defend the entrance to the Solent. Turn right over the bridge to go to the Marine Cafe (dogs outside only) or left before the bridge to the Solent Way along Saltgrass Way. At Keyhaven is The Gun Inn, very dog-friendly (on leads) inside and out. From there you could take the ferry to Hurst Castle, a pleasant boat trip.

WALK 6 CHEWTON COMMON, HIGHCLIFFE

DURATION: *Short walk*

STARTING POINT: *Chewton Common Road*

From Chewton Common Road at the east end of Highcliffe the Common is on the right hand side. One main path takes you to Pinewood Close and the other to Southwood Avenue, but there are smaller paths to explore — a remnant of the New Forest which anciently covered this area.

WALK 7 MUDE RIVER TO MUDEFORD QUAY

DURATION: *Flexible*

STARTING POINT: *Mudeford Community Centre, signposted from The Runway*

FOOD: *Haven House Hotel, Mudeford Quay. Dogs outside only*

From Mudeford Community Centre (toilets here) go straight ahead to a prominent gravel path leaving a copse on your left and walk along the right hand bank of the little River Mude. In September the stream is rather hidden by bracken, pink and white comfrey and other wild flowers but trees screen the walk from a nearby industrial estate which, if the wind is in the right direction wafts the smell of freshly baked bread to whet your appetite! After a few minutes you reach a bridge which you should cross if you only want a short walk (10–15 minutes). It skirts a playing field but there are red bins to clear up if needs be. A longer walk could be taken by starting at The Runway, just past Brabazon Drive and following the grassy area to the Community Centre. Then, instead of crossing the bridge continue on to Mudeford. (You may wonder why the roads are of aeronautical origin. This area was the site of the huge De Haviland aeroplane factory in bygone days and the names echo their products). At the end of the woodland a winding gravel path takes you to the road.

Cross over where you will see the path continuing through mainly birch woodland. At the next road bear slightly right through Osprey Close, an estate of rather nice new houses. The path emerges opposite a large white Fortes hotel. You could continue the walk by turning left here until you reach a red phone box on the opposite side of the road. A path there will take you to Mudeford Quay, well worth a visit with the beautifully situated Haven House Inn at the Avon Run, the narrow entrance to Christchurch harbour. It is pleasant to sit at the tables outside with a drink, snack or meal and watch the waterborne activities. You could then take the little ferryboat across to Mudeford Beach which is dog-friendly and from there on to Hengistbury Head.

WALK 8 BUTTERCUP MEADOW, RINGWOOD

DURATION: *Flexible*
STARTING POINT: *Main (free at time of writing) car park in Ringwood*
FOOD: *Framptons, The Furlong. Dogs outside only*

From the car park take the road alongside Safeways, 'Pedlars Walk'. At the end cross over and follow Kings Arms Lane (by Lloyds Bank) to the end. This emerges at Bickerley Green. A sign reads, 'Avon Valley Path Christchurch 9.5 miles, Salisbury 24.5'. Take the Christchurch path which crosses a bridge over a tributary to the Avon. The water is usually very clear if your dog wants a drink or swim. The walk follows the river valley through watermeadows which, in May and June are usually filled with buttercups which give the walk its name. Walk as far as you like but if you are aiming for Christchurch be warned, as part of this walk is on the road.

WALK 9 MOCKBEGGAR, NEAR RINGWOOD

DURATION: *Flexible*
STARTING POINT: *Mockbeggar Lane*
FOOD: *Alice Lisle Inn, Rockford*

From the Alice Lisle Inn cross the ford to the left and continue for half a mile. Donkeys and New Forest ponies can usually be seen here. Alternatively from the Ringwood-Salisbury road turn right at the little church just before the Old Beams pub into Mockbeggar Lane. A 'no through road' sign leads to the strangely named Mockbeggar. Drive up this until the surface changes to gravel then park considerately as there is a house here. When you reach the top of the track you can take a circular walk by way of the track to the left.

Soon you reach a grassy area with a pond. Head for the group of pines and circle these returning to your starting point. This is a lovely place with wide views, and for longer walks the choice is yours.

WALK 10 RINGWOOD FOREST

DURATION: *Flexible*
STARTING POINT: *Bakers Hanging, B3081*
FOOD: *Alice Lisle, Rockford*
Park at Bakers Hanging on the left, just before the road junction. There are several paths to choose through the pinewoods. Squirrels scamper in the trees and the scents of pines fills the air. This is a favourite walking place for dogs.

WALK 11 ALDERHOLT — EDGE OF RINGWOOD FOREST

DURATION: *Approximately 1 mile*
STARTING POINT: *Bye-road from Ringwood to Alderholt, off B3081*
About 5 miles after Bakers Hanging at Whitefield Bottom park on the left. Turn left at a footpath sign which goes along a grassy/gravel track by two ponds and borders Alderholt Common. After about half a mile the path swings back to the left through pines and circles back to your starting point.

Over to your right is the quaintly named Sleep Brook. Only about a mile in all, but a pleasant walk.

WALK 12 FORDINGBRIDGE

DURATION: ***Short walk***
STARTING POINT: ***Road alongside the George Hotel to sports ground***

From the George Hotel turn right and follow the road to the end before the 'No Entry' signs. Turn right into the car park for the sports ground. This will enable you to take a gentle stroll by the banks of the River Avon. There are views across the river to the old church with weeping willows along the banks. Ducks, moorhens, grebes, swans and coots are usually dabbling in the water in these peaceful surroundings. The cricket ground is behind you with the unmistakably English sound of a match in the season.

WALK 13 SANDY BALLS NATURE TRAIL

DURATION: ***Approximately 1.75 miles***
STARTING POINT: ***Sandy Balls Caravan Park, on B3078 from Fordingbridge***
FOOD: ***Fighting Cocks, Godshill***

This lovely walk through varied terrain of woodland and watermeadows is well worth doing. The start is signposted from the Reception Area of the Caravan Park (which must be one of the most beautifully situated in the area). I will not attempt to describe the walk in detail as it is clearly waymarked. A very good leaflet giving the history of the estate and points to look out for along the way can be obtained from the interesting gift shop for only 20p.

WALK 14 TOYD DOWN

DURATION: ***Approximately 1 hour***
STARTING POINT: ***Half a mile from Tidpit crossroads***
FOOD: ***Fleur de Lys, Cranborne***

From the Cranborne road take the road to Martin. After about 4 miles at Tidpit crossroads go straight over where a sign indicates 'Toyd Down half mile'. Drive on until you reach a large barn and where the paved road ends. Park considerately for the farm machinery making sure not to block any entrances and take the path to the right, just before the barn. There is a wonderful view from here to Martin with its church steeple right across Cranborne Chase. The hill on your right is Windmill Hill and in the vicinity there was a pottery in Roman times. When I researched this walk in December 1997 the grass was crisp with frost and surprisingly, in spite of that a skylark flew up into the clear blue sky as I passed. Turn left at the top of the rise following the waymarker posts. Halfway along the field's edge you will see a signpost

pointing four ways. Take the path to the left. Scattered around are tumuli, ancient burial mounds and as I walked alone with my dog I wondered about the ancients who were buried there. We climbed to the top of a long barrow which gave us even wider views - you'll have to see for yourself! At a green metal gate we turned left which eventually brought us back to a farm track and the barn where our car was parked. (It is worth paying a visit to the village of Martin whilst in the area to see its lovely thatched cottages).

WALK 15 CRICHEL ESTATE WALK TO COCK ROAD

DURATION: *One and a half miles each way*
STARTING POINT: *From B3078 turn left at Horton Inn*
FOOD: *Horton Inn*

Coming from the Horton Inn take the road to Long Crichel. After about 1 mile the road turns right at 90 degrees and on the left is a bridle path across a stream. In December 1997 there was a rickety wooden footbridge here. Follow the bridle path signs through woods and an old driveway for a pleasant, out of this world walk. A cautionary note though, there are many pheasants in the woods so dogs under control please.

WALK 16 HORTON TOWER/QUEENS COPSE/HOLT WOOD

DURATION: *Flexible*
STARTING POINT: *From B3078 turn right at Horton Inn*
FOOD: *Horton Inn*

Visible for miles around, the tower was built in the mid eighteenth century as an observatory. From the Horton Inn drive towards Horton then turn right at the crossroads towards Chalbury. After about half a mile you will see the tower on your left. Park in the small layby on the right and follow the waymarked path which leads uphill past the houses. This goes by the tower which is not open to the public but can be viewed from the ground. Continue along the path and you will come to woodland with plenty of paths to explore.

WALK 17 WEST MOORS PLANTATION

DURATION: *Flexible*
STARTING POINT: *Glenwood Road, West Moors*
FOOD: *Elephant and Castle, West Moors*

Park in Glenwood Road just before the sharp left-hand bend. On your right is a grassy area which leads into quiet pinewoods with more grassy glades. There are many paths to explore, some waymarked, so the choice is yours!

WALK 18 CANNON HILL PLANTATION, COLEHILL

DURATION: *Flexible*
STARTING POINT: *Pilford Heath Road*
FOOD: *Barley Mow Inn, end of Colehill Lane*

The entrance to the woodlands is by a bridle path opposite the end of Cannon Hill Road. The central gravel track widens after about 200 yards and continues to a viewpoint and seat about half a mile in all, but the woods, mainly of pine are very extensive and afford plenty of choice leading eventually to Uddens Plantation. Cannon Hill reputedly got its name from the time of the Civil War and a cannon ball from that period was discovered at nearby Merrifield. The bridle path along the ridge of Cannon Hill was originally part of the route from Hampreston and Little Canford to Colehill.

WALK 19 PYE CORNER/STOUR RIVER WALK, WIMBORNE

DURATION: *Flexible*
STARTING POINT: *Old Road Car Park, Wimborne (charge)*
FOOD: *Vine Inn (small but welcoming); Pudding & Pye Inn*

Between Pudding & Pye Inn and the Green Man is Old Road. Park there and follow the 'no through road'. This leads through allotments to a public footpath 'to Eyebridge'. Across to the left is the many arched Julian's Bridge built in 1636. A fingerboard reads 'Stour Valley Way. Pamphill 1 mile, Wimborne 1.25' You may spot a heron along this stretch. Follow the riverbank until you reach a footpath 'to Pamphill'. Keep following this direction. When you reach the original almshouses and school built in 1698 at Pamphill Green turn right. Follow the line of trees towards a white gate and the entrance to the church. Just past this and having crossed the lane is another footpath sign and stile which will take you to Pamphill Farm Shop. You could take a break here as they have excellent homemade cakes, but it's 'dogs outside only'. Return by the same route to your starting place.

WALK 20 RIVERSIDE POINT, WIMBORNE

DURATION: *Flexible*
STARTING POINT: *Car Park adjoining Brook Road recycling point*
FOOD: *Pudding & Pye Inn, Wimborne*

You can go left to Canford School or right to Station Road. Left will take you under Wimborne bypass and alongside the river. To the right the path is more 'manicured' with an avenue of ornamental trees which are really colourful in the autumn. It is all good runnable grass with views across a quiet stretch of river. At the end of the grassy section to the right there is a high bank with wooden steps leading to the top. This is a viewpoint and will take you along the old railway line (which used to cross the river here. The bridge is now demolished) to Station Road and on market days, Friday Saturday and Sunday, to Wimborne Market. The longer walk to the left will take you past Canford School, parts of which date back to the Norman Conquest and one of the founders of Salisbury Cathedral, William Longspee lived here in 1198. It was the home of Lord Wimborne until 1922 and is now a world famous public school. A longer walk can be taken by continuing along the river bank where oarsmen from the school can often be seen practising, to Stapehill. Various waymarkers will give you the distances and direction.

WALK 21 TARRANT KEYNESTON/BUZBURY RINGS/ ASHLEY WOOD/TARRANT KEYNESTON

DURATION: *Approximately 2 hours*
STARTING POINT: *Tarrant Keyneston Church*
FOOD: *True Lovers Knot, Tarrant Keyneston*
(Can be muddy)

From the B3082 Wimborne to Blandford road turn left to Tarrant Keyneston and park by the church. On the same side and just before the church is a yellow footpath sign and this is where your walk begins. Go uphill along a farm track and on your right are open fields while to the left is a plantation of young trees which in November 1997 were bursting through their protective corsets - or more correctly, deer protection sleeves! Maintain your direc-

tion until you reach a 'delta shaped' yew tree. To your left in the valley is the village of Charlton Marshall on the busy A350 Poole to Blandford road. At the next gateway follow the yellow footpath sign to the right and bear left (keeping the hedge on your left) to some farm buildings with another yellow footpath sign on the gateway in the corner. Go through the gate and turn right leaving the farm buildings on your right. Head for the next gate then through another one close to it. Follow the edge of the field to a stile. Cross it and turn right, continuing alongside the hedge. Go through a very rickety gate and maintain your direction.

In autumn the spindle trees are very pretty with their distinctive pink and orange berries. Pheasants explode from the hedgerows and rabbits bob into their holes along the bridle path. In the field on your right is your first goal, Buzbury Rings. Not much can be seen nowadays, just the outer ring of this Iron Age Fort and Romano British Settlement. To add to its problems it has been bisected by the B3082. Ash trees — the gloriously named *Fraxinus excelsior* — can be seen in the hedgerow and bring to mind an old country saying, 'When the oak is out before the ash we're in for a splash, ash before oak we're in for a soak'! Cross the busy B3082 onto the opposite verge and carry on to your right alongside the golf club.

After a couple of hundred yards there is a tatty (1997) bridle path sign to Tarrant Rushton. Follow its direction, heading for the left hand corner of Ashley Wood which is in front of you. Leave the golf club, keeping the wood on your right and follow the bridleway until it goes into the wood, then you branch left along a grassy track which after about half a mile will take you out to the road. (There is a clear ford almost opposite your exit point if your dog wants a drink or you need to wash off the mud!). Turn right along the lane until you reach the True Lover's Knot. After a break, perhaps, turn right up the hill past two thatched cottages. A footpath is between 'The Hill' and a B & B cottage. Go through but keep your dog on a lead as the current owner of the fields is reputedly very dog unfriendly. Continue past the rear of the cottages emerging finally into the lane near a telephone kiosk. Pass a huge beech tree on your left and in front of you is the church and your starting point.

WALK 22 TARRANT CRAWFORD CIRCULAR WALK

DURATION: *Approximately 1 hour*
STARTING POINT: *100 yards past Tarrant Keyneston Church*
FOOD: *True Lover's Knot, Tarrant Keyneston*

From the B3082 Wimborne to Blandford road turn left to Tarrant Keyneston. About 100 yards past the church, park in a small layby on the left where there is a fingerboard which reads 'T. Crawford 3/4 qtrs mile' When you reach a gate on your left take the path which leads uphill to the left. Pause at the top to see the panoramic views across arable land to Tarrant Keyneston. At the next T junction turn right. Eventually the path reaches a paved lane. A sign reads 'Blandford Forum 3 miles'. Turn right where an old stone cross stands on the corner. (This short section is on the lead). Across to your left you may be able to see Spetisbury Rings, an Iron Age hillfort. At the second gate on your right you will see a stile and bridleway blue marker. Follow the path across the field in line with the electricity poles. At the bottom of the hill on the left are the remains of Tarrant Abbey. Head towards the little twelfth century church in the trees, St Marys Tarrant Crawford. It is usually open and has some striking wall paintings dating from the late 13th century. Fourteen of the scenes depict the life of St Margaret of Antioch, the most extensive in England. Bishop Poore, the builder of Salisbury Cathedral was baptized here. He was Bishop of Salisbury and later Durham and when he was dying expressed the wish to be buried in the abbey he loved. A coffin lid to the north of the altar is reputedly his. Continue along the bridleway following the stream and you will shortly return to your starting place.

WALK 23 QUEENS PARK GOLF COURSE

DURATION: *Flexible*
STARTING POINT: *Queens Park West Drive*

At Queens Park West Drive there is a car park. There are plenty of footpaths around the course and through the wooded areas but care must be taken to avoid golfers. The park extends as far as Queens Park Avenue and is a favourite exercise place for local dogs and their owners.

Walk 25 — Bourne Bottom

WALK 24 FERNHEATH VALLEY SSSI

DURATION: *Short*

STARTING POINT: *Turbary Park Avenue*

At the junction with Fernheath Road you will find a wooded area with a little stream. On the left, partly hidden in undergrowth is a small pond. After a few minutes the path widens out into a meadow. When you reach the end, turn left and the path circles back to a cross roads of paths where you turn right and retrace your steps.

WALK 25 BOURNE BOTTOM, NEAR WALLISDOWN

DURATION: *Flexible*

STARTING POINT: *South Park Road, nr Sainsburys*

This is a pleasant walk by a lake where swans and ducks rear their young in Spring. For the adventurous, it is just possible to walk around the lake (although the bracken can be a hazard in July/August). Otherwise the grassy stretch leads along the valley following the Bourne Stream which gave Bournemouth its name. The walk eventually emerges at the busy Ringwood Road so it would be advisable to retrace your steps to South Park Road.

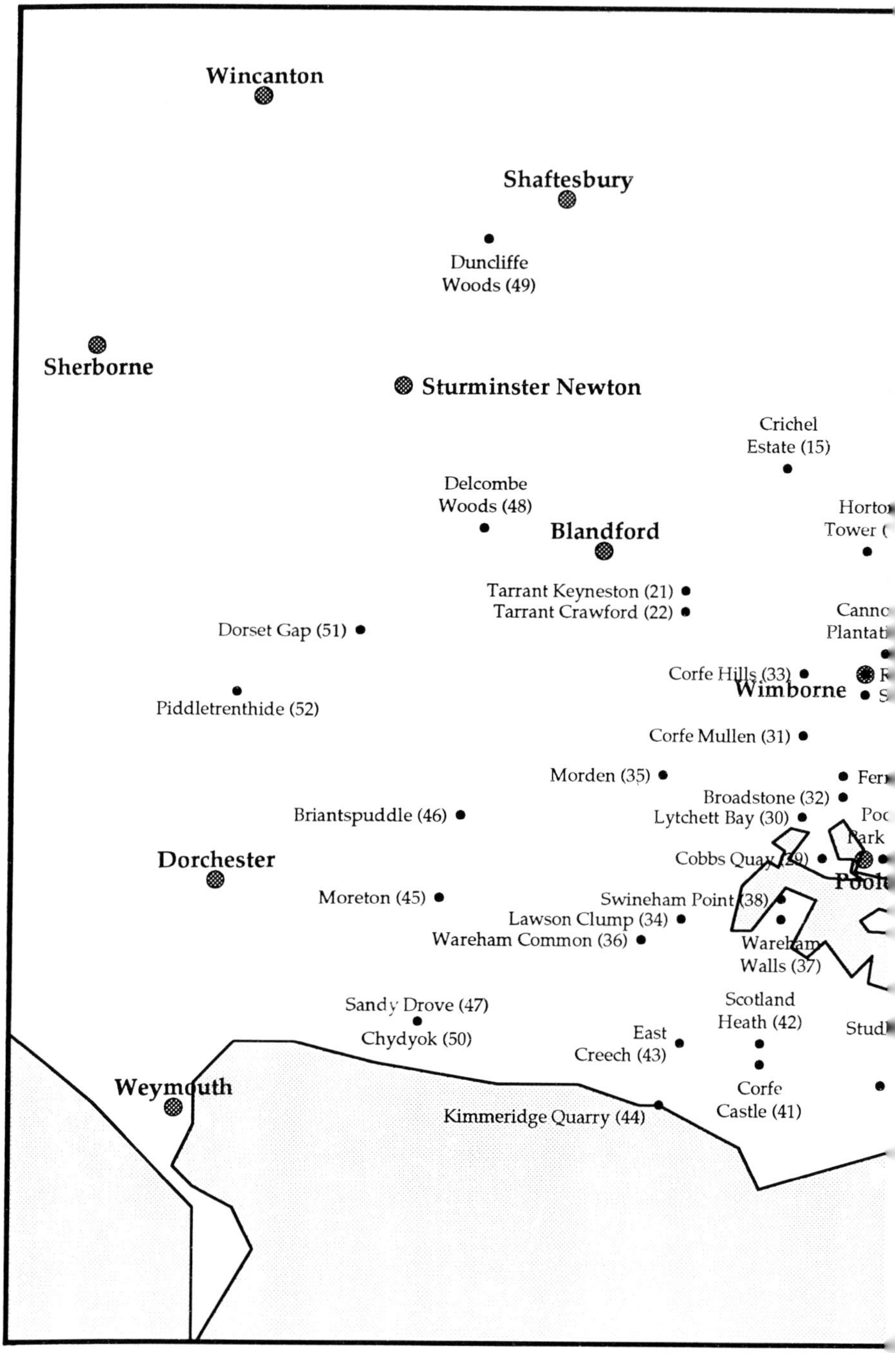
Wincanton
Shaftesbury
Duncliffe Woods (49)
Sherborne
Sturminster Newton
Crichel Estate (15)
Delcombe Woods (48)
Blandford
Tarrant Keyneston (21)
Tarrant Crawford (22)
Dorset Gap (51)
Piddletrenthide (52)
Corfe Hills (33)
Wimborne
Corfe Mullen (31)
Morden (35)
Broadstone (32)
Briantspuddle (46)
Lytchett Bay (30)
Dorchester
Cobbs Quay (29)
Moreton (45)
Swineham Point (38)
Lawson Clump (34)
Wareham Common (36)
Wareham Walls (37)
Sandy Drove (47)
Chydyok (50)
Scotland Heath (42)
East Creech (43)
Weymouth
Corfe Castle (41)
Kimmeridge Quarry (44)

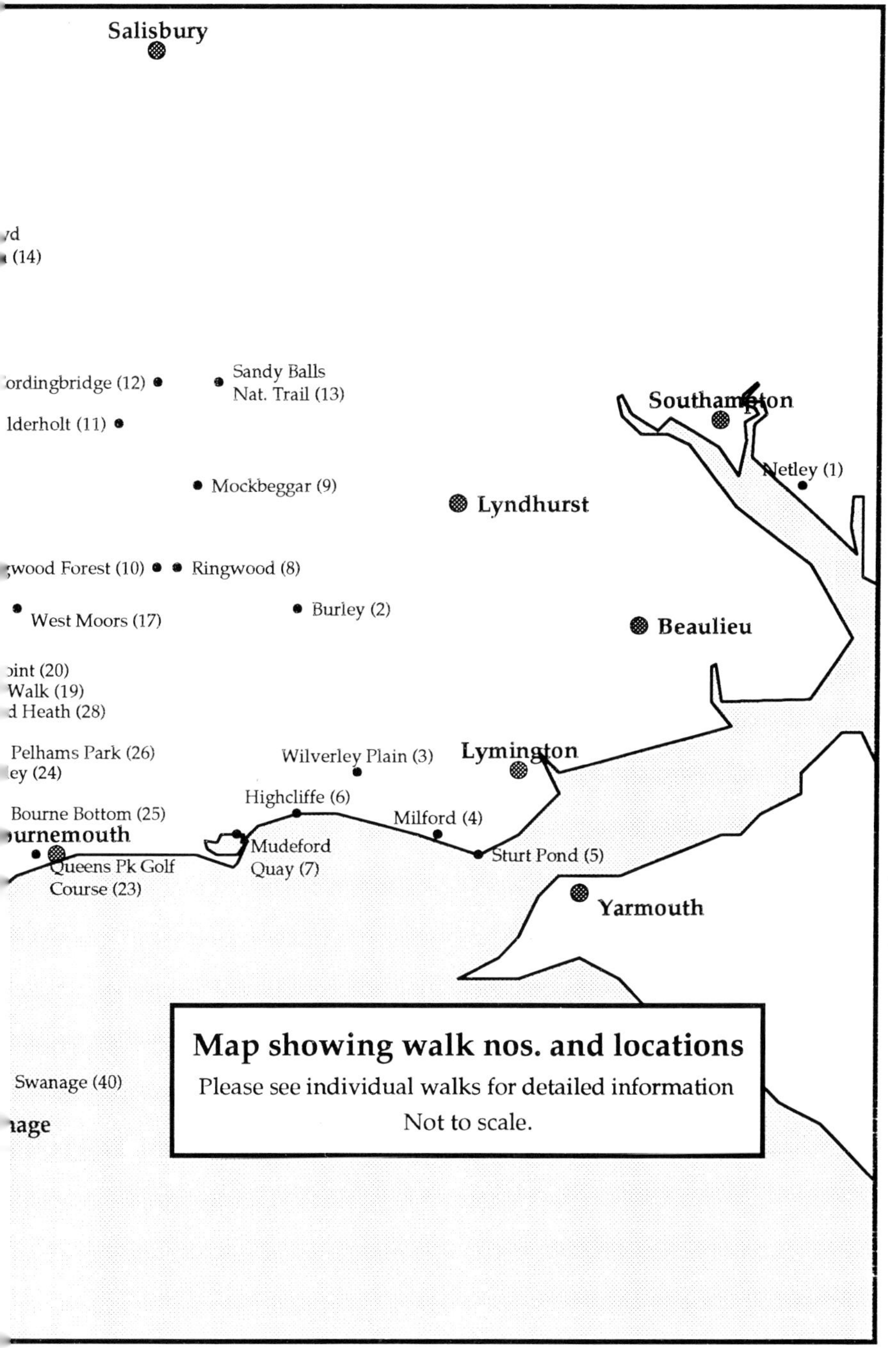

Map showing walk nos. and locations

Please see individual walks for detailed information

Not to scale.

WALK 26 PELHAMS PARK, KINSON

DURATION: *Short*

STARTING POINT: *Pelhams Park*

From Wimborne Road, Kinson turn right into Millhams Road. Just past Weymans Avenue on the right is Pelhams House, now a community centre. Its grassy grounds which include a large holm oak, tulip tree and plane tree are open to the public and will provide a pleasant short walk. Pelhams House, a well-proportioned Georgian structure was built in 1793 and reputed to be the home of Isaac Gulliver, Dorset's most famous smuggler. Later it belonged to Rev. Canon Arnold Sharp, vicar of Kinson and in 1930 was bought by Bournemouth Corporation for the benefit of the people of Kinson.

WALK 27 POOLE PARK/BAITER/WHITECLIFF

DURATION: *Flexible*

STARTING POINT: *Copse Close, off Orchard Avenue*

FOOD: *Swan Lake, Poole Park, dogs outside only; Kiosk at Baiter in summer*

Alongside Copse Close is a grassy area with old oak and other broad-leaved trees which is safe off the lead but as you approach the Freshwater Lake with its ducks, swans and geese plus miniature railway it is safer 'on the lead' for all concerned! A footpath wends its way following the narrow railtrack behind and to the left of the lake and you emerge by the majestic eagles topping the entrance gateposts with their dolphin panels. Go through the gateway alongside the larger saltwater lake. The enclosed area is for model boats and it is fun to watch the enthusiasts sailing them there. Continue on under the tiny railway bridge and just afterwards on your right is a gateway leading into the open grasslands of Whitecliff and Baiter. Poole Quay can be reached off lead by walking to the right along the shoreline. There are fine views of Poole Harbour, the islands and shipping large and small.

WALK 28 CANFORD HEATH, BRIDLEWAY TO ALDERNEY

DURATION: *Flexible*
STARTING POINT: *Layby near Poole Crematorium*
This is signposted from the entrance to the Crematorium on the roundabout between Fleets Bridge and Wimborne but it is easier to park at the layby on the right before the roundabout. There is an entrance to the Heath via some steps. Keep following the path to the left parallel with but a safe distance from the busy road for about 200–300 yards, then you will meet the wide bridleway going uphill. Follow this and you will find great views across Tower Park, Poole and the Purbeck Hills. The path continues to Alderney but the Heath covers a large area from Poole to Wimborne so you can detour on to other paths at will. A pleasant walk and a favourite with dogs and their owners. In ancient times the cattle belonging to the townspeople of Poole were driven out here by day to graze.

WALK 29 COBBS QUAY, HAMWORTHY

DURATION: *Approximately 25 minutes each way*
STARTING POINT: *Corner Hinchcliffe Road/Woodlands Avenue*
FOOD: *Courtyard Centre, Lytchett Minster. Dogs outside only but some cover*
A sign shows 'FP108 to Foreshore'. Follow this, then FP12 to the left — the going can be a bit rough — past private jetties. This takes you under oak trees along the foreshore. The masts of craft at Cobbs Quay Marina are ahead. You should pass pretty back gardens of houses, reed beds and mudflats. At the electricity pylons take the footpath through wire-netted gates back to the road where you continue past Cobbs Quay entrance. Turn right at the corner then right again to the foreshore for the prettiest part of the walk which could be taken separately. Panoramic views lead the eye across Holes Bay towards Tower Park, Parkstone Heights, Longfleet Church and Upton Park. There are plenty of doggy bins by the tarmac path. A sign on one house reads, 'Thank you for cleaning up after your dog'. At the end of the shoreline path by a galleon weathervane you meet a road, so retrace your steps at that point.

WALK 30 LYTCHETT BAY, SHORE LANE, UPTON

DURATION: *Short walk*

STARTING POINT: *Sandy Lane*

From Hamworthy take the Blandford Road to Upton. Sandy Lane is on your left, just a few hundred yards past the Turlin Moor traffic lights. Shore Lane is the second turning left off Sandy Lane. Drive to the end and you will see a grassy footpath which will take you to the shore of Lytchett Bay. This is a very pretty spot when the tide is in with views across the bay that visitors could easily miss. The bridge ahead is Rockley Viaduct which carries the railway line from Dorchester to Poole. There are a couple of short but pleasant paths to choose from. The land across the bay to your right leads to Holton Heath where there was a large Cordite factory in World War Two. Decca Records were also there but from this viewpoint no trace remains. A 350 acre holiday centre for the disabled, 'Holton Lee' now has its base in this lovely area.

WALK 31 CORFE MULLEN VIEWPOINT, UPTON HEATH

DURATION: *Flexible*

STARTING POINT: *Car park, Corfe Mullen end of Springdale Road*

A gravel track from the car park leads in about 500 yards to the viewpoint where, on a clear day there is a fantastic panoramic view from the Isle of Wight to Bulbarrow which encompasses the whole of Poole Harbour, the Purbeck hills and Wareham channel. The walk can be extended over Upton Heath or a shorter circuit may be made by taking the rough track around the waterworks and back to the car park. Binoculars recommended!

WALK 32 POCKET PARK, BROADSTONE

DURATION: *Short walk*

STARTING POINT: *Lower Blandford Road*

Half way down Lower Blandford Road from Broadstone to the roundabout is Pocket Park. It lies between Wallace Road and Edwina Drive and consists of rough grass with scattered bushes. Small, but a favourite exercise place for dogs.

WALK 33 CORFE HILLS, BROADSTONE GOLF COURSE

DURATION: *Approximately 0.75 of a mile*

STARTING POINT: *Side road opposite Corfe Hills School, Higher Blandford Road. Park on the verge or the side road opposite the school*

Go through the golf course gate and cross the 13th fairway on the lead as golfers may be approaching from your left.The track is gravelled, level and a pleasant stroll with seats along the way. The golf course limits are marked

by white posts and within these you are permitted to walk. A dirt track, kinder to dogs paws, runs parallel to the gravel for much of the way. You can circle to the left through roughish ground behind teasels where there is an active rabbit warren with its tantalising scents for your dog. To the far east seemingly endless woods extend to the New Forest while to the north are glimpses of the Wiltshire Downs. It is at its best when gorse and heather are in bloom and to be appreciated should be taken on a day of good visibility. Thirty years ago the main path continued to Merley but since being purchased by the golf club the right of way ends at the old railway line.

WALK 34 LAWSON CLUMP, WAREHAM FOREST

DURATION: *Flexible*

STARTING POINT: *Lawson Clump car park, B3075*

From the A35 Poole to Dorchester road turn left towards Wareham at Morden Park Corner on the B3075. About 2.5 miles on the left is a car park with the sign, 'Lawson Clump', surrounded by Lawsonii trees. From here there are many walks to choose through the pinewoods of Gore Heath. The paths are generally good, gravel or sand but you may encounter the odd muddy patch after wet weather. Don't get lost though, as some paths look very like another!

Walk 34 — Lawson Clump

WALK 35 MORDEN PARK CORNER

DURATION: ***Short walk, approximately 15 minutes each way***
STARTING POINT: ***A35, Morden Park Corner***
FOOD: ***Cock and Bottle, Morden***

On either side heading towards Bere Regis there is a small layby on the brow of the hill soon after Morden Park Corner cross roads. On the right a waymarker reads 'Morden 1.5 miles, Wareham Forest Way' and on the left 'Wareham Forest Way, Wareham 5.75 miles'. This walk is on the right where a sandy track leads through bracken and woodland and a tunnel of trees where the path is grassy. Rabbits and pheasants abound! At Hectors Corner (houses) we turned round as the walk continues along the road to Morden.

WALK 36 WAREHAM COMMON VIA CAREY TO SILENT WOMAN, COLDHARBOUR

DURATION: ***Approximately 1 3/4 hours each way***
STARTING POINT: ***West Walls car park***
FOOD: ***Silent Woman***

From the end of the car park furthest from the main road follow the footpath on to the Common. Continue under the road and railway bridges and follow the track towards and behind a large whitish barn. Keep on this path, following the footpath signs. At Carey you cross a road and keep straight on. The path goes through pinewoods and eventually emerges approximately

100 yards from the Silent Woman which is on your left. (The Silent Woman is so called because she carries her head under her arm!). After a break at the pub, retrace your steps to Wareham. A very pleasant walk.

WALK 37 WAREHAM WALLS

DURATION: *Approximately 3/4 qtrs of an hour*
STARTING POINT: *Wareham Quay car park*
FOOD: *Old Granary, The Quay. Dogs outside only. Antelope Inn*

Built by King Alfred in the 9th century the walls surround the town on three sides, the 4th being protected by the River Frome. This walk can be joined at any point and takes you along the top of the walls which are earthen banks covered in wild flowers in summer. If you start from the Quay, go past Lady St Mary's church and you will find 'Walls Walk' well signposted. Points of interest along the way are the Bowling Green, an open grassy area near the River Piddle — possibly a post medieval enclosure and part of a pleasure garden. Fairs were held here in the 18th century. 'Bloody Bank', near the Streche Road car park at West Walls was the place of execution in bygone days.

WALK 38 WAREHAM TO SWINEHAM POINT

DURATION: *Approximately 2 hours*

STARTING POINT: *2 choices: 1. from rear of churchyard: 2. From Bestwall Rd just past Bestwall Crescent 1. Includes a little roadwork. 2. Footpath signposted 'To river, and a little further on, 'To Swineham'*

The walk takes you through watermeadows and along the northern bank of the River Frome. With its moored craft and passing yachts there is always something to enchant the eye. Glimpses of waterfowl can be seen through the reeds and ever present in the distance are the Purbeck Hills. About a quarter of the way along you may spot Redcliffe Farm made famous in a painting by the eminent Cornish artist Lamorna Birch, and then at the half-way stage you may see the masts at Ridge Wharf on the opposite side of the river. From then onwards to the Point the path can be rather overgrown with reeds at times — not pleasant if they are wet and you are not prepared! Just before the Point the path turns sharp left which would take you back to Wareham on a slightly shorter route. If you continue, the footpath cuts across the Point where the fields end and the marshes begin — a favourite spot for birdwatchers — and then follow the waymarked path which is straight and grassy, back to Bestwalls Road. An interesting walk. Swineham Point is where the River Frome enters Poole Harbour. In ancient times Wareham was the busiest port in the area but then the river began to silt up and larger craft could no longer reach Wareham Quay. It was then that Poole took over as the major port of the harbour, and Wareham's trade decreased.

WALK 39 WOODHOUSE (STUDLAND) TO THE SEA

DURATION: *Short walk*

STARTING POINT: *Just outside Studland on Swanage road*

At this location a layby with an advertisment for the Bankes Arms Hotel is the place to park. A pleasant footpath follows the line of the hedge downhill to the sea. In bygone days it was used by folk trading with pirates on the seashore!

WALK 40 SWANAGE (ULWELL) TO CORFE CASTLE

DURATION: *3.5 miles*

STARTING POINT: *Layby near Waterworks at Ulwell*

FOOD: *Greyhound Inn, Fox Inn, Corfe Castle*

A short distance back up the hill you will see a waymarker on the left, '3.5 miles to Corfe Castle'. The first hill is Nine Barrow Down with its Bronze Age burial chambers and which legend says cover the graves of nine kings killed in battle. Below you is Godlingston Manor, parts of which date from the 13th century. Next is Brenscombe, then East Hill and from there you descend to Corfe Castle. A wonderful walk.

WALK 41 CORFE CASTLE NATIONAL TRUST CAR PARK TO VILLAGE

DURATION: *Short walk*
STARTING POINT: *National Trust car park. (Free 1997)*

Cross the busy A351 with care and take the newly opened footpath to the village, thereby avoiding the noisy traffic. You will pass the ruins of West Mill (excavated Spring 1998) which goes back many hundreds of years. Cross the minor road and take the footpath around the base of the castle mound and alongside the little Corfe River, previously part of the moat. This emerges by the castle entrance. (Dogs on lead permitted in the castle). The village is very picturesque. Don't miss the cottages in West Street beyond the other car park. (If you are interested, my historical novel *The Bountifull Gyfte* set in Corfe Castle and Purbeck in Elizabethan times and based on fact is on sale in the village).

WALK 42 CORFE CASTLE TO SCOTLAND HEATH

DURATION: *Short walk*
STARTING POINT: *National Trust car park, outskirts of village on A351*
FOOD: *Marblers Cafe (not Mon); Greyhound Inn; Fox Inn; Moretons House Hotel*

From the National Trust car park take the footpath to Norden Park & Ride alongside the steam railway line and follow the waymarker posts to Scotland Heath. This walk takes you through trees, heath and grassy tracts and is a pleasant break if you are returning by train to Swanage.

WALK 43 EAST CREECH TO CORFE CASTLE

DURATION: *Approximately 1 hour each way*
STARTING POINT: *Near East Creech Farm Caravan Park*
FOOD: *Marblers Cafe (not Mon); Fox Inn; Greyhound Inn*

From the A351 take the turning off the roundabout to Blue Pool. Continue on past and just before East Creech Farm Caravan Park but on the left is a small parking space with footpath signs. Take the one to Corfe Castle and Norden Farm. This goes through very pretty undulating woodland with unexpected pools on either side. The shape of the land is due to clayworking in bygone days, but the scars have now healed to give a picturesque walk. If you keep following the waymarkers to Corfe Castle you could see interesting wildlife at any time of the year. When you reach the village, take a break at one of the hostelries, have a look around, then retrace your steps. We always enjoy this walk.

WALK 44 KIMMERIDGE QUARRY TO SWYRE HEAD

DURATION: *Approximately 1 1/2 hours return*
STARTING POINT: *Disused quarry before road branches to Smedmore/Kimmeridge*
FOOD: *7 Taps Kimmeridge. Dogs outside only; Scott Arms, Kingston*

On leaving the quarry turn right, then right again and go up the rough farm track and footpath which takes you along the ridge. (There may be sheep or cattle in the fields. If so, dogs on leads please). It is a bit of a climb but the views when you reach Swyre Head are almost too beautiful - the ever changing moods of clouds, the craggy Dorset coastline, across Poole Harbour, the cliffs of Bournemouth, the Isle of Wight and Portland - all spread out before you. On a very clear day reputedly the Cherbourg Peninsular can be seen with binoculars if you focus to the right of the wooden seat on the headland. Having had your fill, retrace your steps or for a longer walk take the route above the 'Golden Bowl of Encombe' past Polar Wood and thence to Kingston. A beautiful walk and certainly worth the effort.

WALK 45 MORETON TO OAKERS WOOD, etc

DURATION: *Flexible*
STARTING POINT: *'No through road' leading to river by P.O. shop*
FOOD: *Royal Oak, Bere Regis*

A footbridge crosses the River Frome where ducks sport themselves in the clear shallows. A straightish track runs between rhododendron bushes and trees emerging finally at the road. If you wish to cross over into Oakers Wood you could continue along the waymarked Jubilee Trail to Culpeppers Dish (see Walk 46). Moreton has two main claims to fame: Lawrence of Arabia's grave is in the cemetery and the windows of the church of St Nicholas were beautifully engraved by Lawrence Whistler in 1958 — well worth a visit.

WALK 46 CULPEPPERS DISH TO BRIANTSPUDDLE FOREST

DURATION: *Flexible*
STARTING POINT: *Culpeppers Dish car park, near Briantspuddle*

From the left corner of the car park take the unmarked footpath leading downhill. After a couple of hundred yards it meets a wider track where you turn right. This is Briantspuddle Forest on the Jubilee Trail where you can explore at will. If you want to go to Moreton, follow the bridle path. There are conifers, a pond with waterlilies and pleasant views along the way. If you keep bearing right and follow the red posts for a circular walk you will come to a sign which says 'car park to left'. Caution, this is not where you parked. Yours is on the right. A quiet, safe off lead walk.

WALK 47 SANDY DROVE

DURATION: *Short, but could be extended*
STARTING POINT: *A352, near turning to East Chaldon*
FOOD: *Sailors Return, East Chaldon*

From the A352 there is a short (half mile) but pleasant walk to the top of the hill from which there are sweeping views in all directions. This walk could be extended by turning right to the Five Marys, tumuli or burial mounds about half a mile further on.

WALK 48 DELCOMBE WOODS

DURATION: *Flexible*
STARTING POINT: *Turnworth to Bulbarrow road*

From the Turnworth to Bulbarrow road take the turning to Milton Abbas and after 1 mile you will see a gateway on the right, just past Delcombe Manor with its long flintstone boundary walls. A sign in the gateway reads, 'Walkers welcome here. Forest Enterprise'. What a pleasant surprise when dog owners are so often banned! Ancient woodland surrounds you with yews and broadleaved trees. There are several tracks to left and right to choose from but some can be muddy. In spring, bluebells abound here.

WALK 49 DUNCLIFFE WOOD

DURATION: *Flexible*
STARTING POINT: *Half mile down rd opp Kings Arms, A30, 4 m from Shaftesbury*
FOOD: *Kings Arms, East Stour*

Opposite the inn a sign reads 'Stour Row 1½ miles'. Half a mile down the road on the left is the entrance to the wood. A sign , 'Woodland Trust. Visitors are welcome to walk in our woods ' greets you. They ask that dogs be under control as there are deer there. A dry, gravelled path leads alongside two fields to the wood which is on a hill and can be seen for miles around. Wild strawberries grow on ancient mossy banks and there are plenty of paths for walkers with dogs to explore although horse riders are restricted. Glimpses of Thomas Hardy's Vale of Dairies, ie Blackmore Vale can be seen through the trees. This walk is recommended, especially in bluebell time.

WALK 50 CHYDYOK, EAST CHALDON

DURATION: *Approximately one hour*
STARTING POINT: *The village green*
FOOD: *Sailors Return, East Chaldon*

From the village green head uphill into Chydyok Road cul-de-sac past the estate houses. At the end of the road go through the gate and up a gravel track. A board tells you the land is open under the Countryside Stewards

Scheme and a map shows where you are permitted to walk. A bit of a stiff climb but worth it for the views to Winfrith, Five Marys and into Dorset's heartland. Just over the crest of the hill, go through a gate and turn left. This takes you downhill through a lovely grassy valley where time stands still. Field boundaries dating back to 1000BC are still visible today. Much of this land has not been ploughed since Roman times, resulting in plentiful wild flowers in spring and summer. At the bottom of the valley a stone is inscribed 'East Chaldon 1/2 mile' to the left, 'Daggers Gate 1 mile'. Turn left. When you reach the road turn left again and walk through the village. The Dorset Queen coach depot is on your right and the village green ahead. A most enjoyable walk - especially if there are no sheep in the grassy valley and your dog can explore freely.

WALK 51 DORSET GAP, NR MELCOMBE BINGHAM

DURATION: *Allow 2 hours*
STARTING POINT: *Cross Lanes crossroads, Melcombe Bingham*
FOOD: *Fox Inn, Anstey*

From Melcombe Bingham drive through the village to Cross Lanes crossroads. Park considerately near the houses then walk up the lane to Higher Melcombe. Partly hidden in the hedge on your left is a waymarker post which reads 'Dorset Gap 1½ miles' but that distance indicates the direct route. After about 5 minutes walk along the lane, you come to a rather ornate wrought iron sign which says 'Private Road'. On the right is a gateway with a blue bridleway and yellow footpath sign. Take the yellow track which goes up a very steep grassy hill. The path follows the hedge to the left and soon you will see fine views across the rolling hills and downland of Dorset. Head towards the woods as indicated by a finger post. Through a steep gulley there are many wild flowers - orchids, cowslips and primroses in their season. Maintain your direction through an iron gate and you will find another waymarker post pointing in various directions. Just past this on the right is a green box inscribed 'Dorset Gap' . Inside is a tin box with notebooks going back over the years for visitors to write their comments. (If you can find 30 June 1997 you will see ours!). Walk towards Folly then take the track downhill to the left and follow the blue bridle path signs back to the lane, emerging about 100 yards from where you entered. There is an avenue of young copper beech trees on the right of the lane, which takes you back to your starting point.

WALK 52 PLUSH, NEAR PIDDLETRENTHIDE

DURATION: *Flexible*

STARTING POINT: *Brace of Pheasants*

FOOD: *Brace of Pheasants. Very pleasant & dog friendly - but carpeted so no muddy boots please!*

Plush is reached from the Dorchester to Piddletrenthide road. At Piddletrenthide a turning sharp right and steeply uphill is signposted 'Plush' and 'Brace of Pheasants'. After about 10 minutes drive you reach the village. About 100 yards to the left of the pub as you face it is a cart track leading uphill. A bridleway sign reads 'to Alton Pancras 1¼ miles' alongside the village sign, 'Plush' and this is where your walk begins. Ancient earthworks abound on the surrounding hills. This really is a lovely walk. Buzzards can often be seen circling overhead. Ignore the footpath to the left and continue on the bridleway. On top of the hill is a gate. Go through and like us you will probably gasp at the explosion of a view to the valley falling steeply to your right. By the gate is a map showing the permitted access under the Countryside Stewards scheme — and you will be spoilt for choice. I would recommend carrying straight ahead to the gate in the distance as there is yet another panoramic view from here, and another map. I also suggest exploring the little village street after visiting the pub with its stuffed brace of pheasants as a sign. There is Gardeners Cottage, Prisoners Cottage (what is the origin of that, I wonder?) and in a cul-de-sac more thatch with very steeply pitched roofs. The Inn was originally a smithy and a pair of thatched cottages. There was a disastrous fire here in the 1970s but no sign of it remains due to careful restoration. A lovely walk.

THINGS TO DO ACCOMPANIED BY YOUR DOG

LYMINGTON TO YARMOUTH ISLE OF WIGHT..... ..... & A WALK TO FRESHWATER

Ferries run every half an hour or so throughout the year. It is expensive to take your car but you can park it at Lymington Ferry Terminal and travel as a foot passenger. No charge for dogs. Enjoy the views of Lymington River, Hurst Castle and the shores of the IOW. The stumpy tower of Yarmouth church is straight ahead. When you disembark, go straight ahead to the large car park where you will find a footpath leading to the right along an old railway track. This follows the Yar Estuary and emerges at Old Freshwater village. Next to the church is the Red Lion, an Egon Ronay recommended pub and IOW Dining Pub of the Year - and they are very dog-friendly! If you have the time and inclination you could continue along the footpath to Freshwater Bay or alternatively follow the waymarker posts to the west of the Yar Estuary which will bring you back to Yarmouth and the ferry. This makes a lovely day out.

SWANAGE TO CORFE CASTLE BY STEAM RAILWAY

Trains run frequently throughout the season with various special offers (see Swanage Station for details) Relive the Golden Age of Steam and travel through Purbeck to Corfe Castle. This pretty village with its castle ruins dominating the scene is well worth a visit and there are walks to do once they have been explored. Alongside 19 West Street is a footpath which leads through fields called 'The Halves' or it is worth walking to the end of West Street with its attractive cottages to the Common where time stands still. Wild flowers grow in profusion, while horses, donkeys and cattle graze as their ancestors have done for centuries. See the list for choice of dog friendly eating places.

MUTMOBILE & BRATMOBILE BIKE HIRE, BURLEY

In Burley village near the pub is the Mutmobile and Bratmobile Bike Hire Co where you can hire cycle trailers designed to carry your dog and another for your child — a novel way to explore the New Forest if you have an elderly or lazy pet! Telephone 01425 403584 for details.

MacPENNY'S NURSERY. CHOICE & RARE PLANTS, PLUS WALK, BRANSGORE

This is a popular plantsmans nursery which sells choice and rare plants. The attraction is that they have many of them growing in their landscaped wooded garden where you can walk with your dog and admire the plants in their natural habitat. A pleasant way to spend an hour or so.

COURTYARD CENTRE, LYTCHETT MINSTER

This is signposted from the Upton to Lytchett Minster road and also from the Upton to Blandford road. The Centre was a collection of old stables and they have been converted to small shops and workshops where in some cases you can see the crafts taking place. There is a cafe/restaurant but dogs are not allowed inside. However they now have an outside area with a tented roof where you may sit and eat with your dog. There is also a garden centre and a pets corner but dogs are not allowed in the latter as there are rabbits and poultry.

DOG FRIENDLY PUBS AND EATING PLACES

Dogs allowed inside on lead (See 'FOOD' section at beginning of book).

1 **NORTH HAMPSHIRE AREA**
Greyhound, Stockbridge

2 **NEW FOREST AREA**
High Corner Inn, Linwood
Red Shoot Inn, Linwood
Foresters Arms, Abbotswell
New Queen, Avon
Three Tuns, Bransgore
Amberwood Hotel, Walkford
Royal Oak, Bank
Foresters Arms, Brockenhurst
Fighting Cocks, Godshill
New Forest Inn, Emery Down
White Buck, Burley
Burley Manor Hotel, Burley
Hare and Hounds, Sway

3 **COASTAL AREA, EAST OF BOURNEMOUTH**
Ship in Distress, Stanpit
The Mayflower, Lymington
Beachcomber Cafe & Restaurant, Barton on Sea
The Master Builder, Bucklers Hard
Smugglers Inn, Milford on Sea
The Gun, Keyhaven

4 **COASTAL AREA, WEST OF BOURNEMOUTH**
Bankes Arms, Studland
Durlston Castle, Durlston Head
Old Castle Inn, Castle Cove, Weymouth
George Hotel, Reforne, Portland
Little Ship, Chiswell
New Inn, Eype

5 **PURBECK AREA, INLAND**
Antelope Hotel, Wareham
Horse & Groom, Wareham
Marblers Cafe, Corfe Castle
Greyhound Inn, Corfe Castle
Fox Inn, Corfe Castle
Moretons House Hotel, Corfe Castle
Scott Arms, Kingston

6 **EAST DORSET AREA, INLAND**
The Drovers, Gussage All Saints
Horton Inn, Horton
Greyhound, Winterborne Kingston
Royal Oak, Okeford Fitzpaine
White Horse Inn, Stourpaine
Stepping Stones, Broadstone
Silent Woman, Coldharbour
Cock and Bottle, Morden
Fleur de Lys, Cranborne
Milton Arms, Winterborne Whitchurch
Royal Oak, Bere Regis
Greyhound, Blandford
Crown Hotel, Blandford
Alices Cafe, Parkstone
Barley Mow, Colehill

7 **DORSET/WILTSHIRE BORDER**
The Forester, Donhead
Rising Sun, Donhead
King John Inn, Tollard Royal
Kings Arms, East Stour

8 **CENTRAL/WEST DORSET**
The Springhead, Sutton Poyntz
Cornwall Hotel, Dorchester
Sailors Return, East Chaldon
Royal Oak, Cerne Abbas

ONCE AGAIN — HAPPY WALKIES!